Poems about

Day & Night

Selected by
Amanda Earl & Danielle Sensier

Illustrated by
Frances Lloyd

Wayland

Titles in the series
Poems about . . .

Animals	**Food**
Colours	**Growth**
Day & Night	**Homes**
Families	**Journeys**
Feelings	**Weather**

For David, Rebecca, Rachael and Joanna

King's Road Primary School
Rosyth - Tel: 313470

Series editor: Catherine Baxter
Designer: Loraine Hayes

First published in 1995 by
Wayland (Publishers) Ltd
61 Western Road, Hove
East Sussex BN3 1JD, England

© Copyright 1995 Wayland
(Publishers) Ltd

British Library Cataloguing in Publication Data

Poems About Day and Night. – (Poems
About . . . Series)
   I. Earl, Amanda II. Sensier, Danielle
   III. Series
   808.8133

   ISBN 0-7502-1125-3

Front cover design: S. Balley

Typeset by Dorchester Typesetting
Group Ltd., Dorset, England.
Printed and bound in Italy by
G. Canale & C.Sp.A., Turin.

Poets' nationalities

Jean Little	Canadian
Karla Kuskin	American
Pauline Stewart	British/Jamaican
Shirley Hughs	English
Clive Sansom	English
Robert Frost	American
Eleanor Farjeon	English
Judith Viorst	American

Contents

My Own Day

When I opened my eyes this morning,
The day belonged to me.
The sky was mine and the sun,
And my feet got up dancing.
The marmalade was mine and the squares of sidewalk
And all the birds in the trees.
So I stood and I considered
Stopping the world right there,
Making today go on and on forever.
But I decided not to.
I let the world spin on and I went to school.
I almost did it, but then, I said to myself,
"Who knows what you might be missing tomorrow?"

Jean Little

Song to Bring Fair Weather

You, whose day it is, make it beautiful.
Get out your rainbow colours,
So it will be beautiful.

Nootka People, North America

4

Very Early

When I wake in the early mist
The sun has hardly shown
And everything is still asleep
And I'm awake alone.
The stars are faint and flickering.
The sun is new and shy.
And all the world sleeps quietly,
Except the sun and I.
And then the noises start,
The whirrs and huffs and hums,
The birds peep out to find a worm.
The mice squeak out for crumbs,
The calf moos out to find the cow,
And taste the morning air
And everything is wide awake
And running everywhere.
The dew has dried,
The fields are warm,
The day is loud and bright,
And I'm the one who woke the sun
And kissed the stars good night.

Karla Kuskin

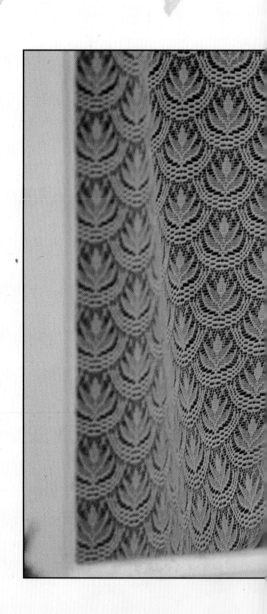

In the Morning

In the morning
a little bird
that has no name
flies westward
pulling away
the dark blanket of the night.

Siv Cedering Fox

On a blue day

On a blue day
when the brown heat
scorches the grass
and stings my legs with sweat

I go running like a fool
up the hill towards the trees
and my heart beats loudly,
like a kettle boiling dry.

I need a bucket the size of the sky
filled with cool, cascading water.

At evening
the cool air rubs my back,
I listen to the bees
working for their honey

and the sunset pours light
over my head like a waterfall.

David Harmer

Late for breakfast

Who is it hides my sandals when I'm trying
to get dressed?
And takes away the hairbrush that was lying
on the chest?
I wanted to start breakfast before any of the
others
But something's always missing, or been
borrowed by my brothers.
I think I'd better dress at night, and eat my
breakfast too,
Then when everybody's hurrying –
I'll have nothing else to do.

Mary Jeffries

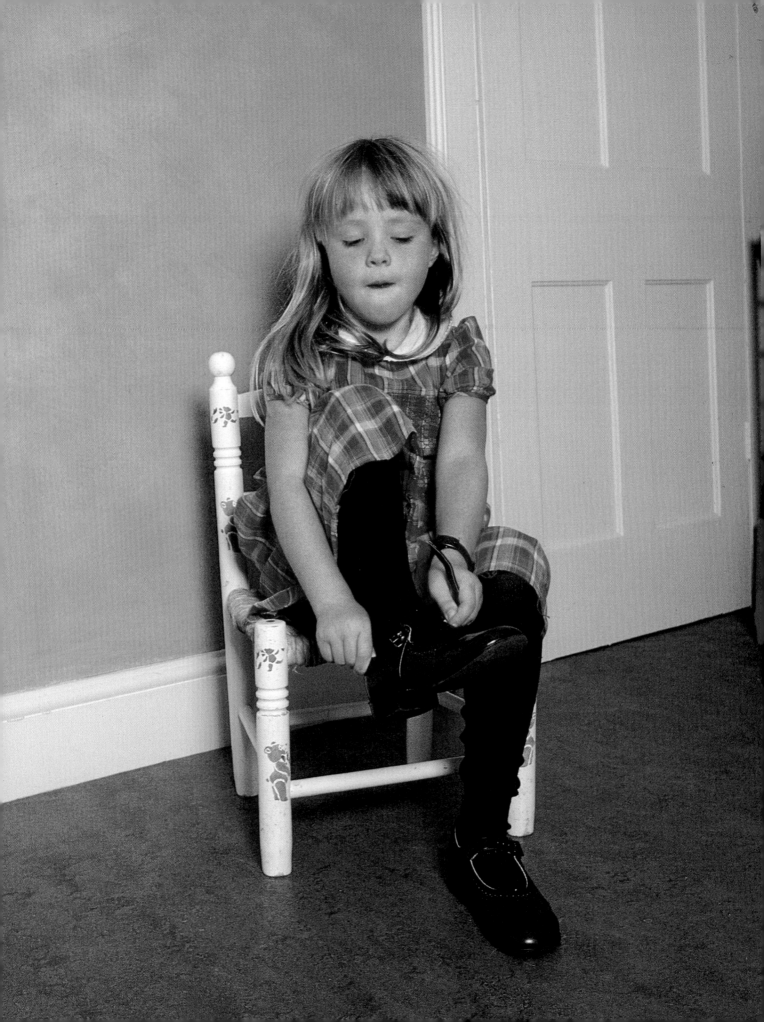

The Spinning Earth

The earth, they say,
spins round and round.
It doesn't look it
from the ground,
and never makes
a spinning sound.

And water never
swirls and swishes
from oceans full
of dizzy fishes,
and shelves don't lose
their pans and dishes.

And houses don't go whirling by,
or puppies swirl around the sky,
or robins spin instead of fly.

It may be true
what people say
about one spinning
night and day . . . .
but I keep wondering, anyway.

Aileen Fisher

13

Washday

In the sun we scrips our clothes
and everyone around us knows
that soon our sheets will sail the wind
flap and flutter, twirl like string.
Our tops and bottoms look like flags
hung on a line which gently sags.
The washday chore is almost done
my jeans dry quickly in the sun.

Pauline Stewart

Seaside

Sand in the sandwiches,
Sand in the tea,
Flat, wet sand running
Down to the sea.
Pools full of seaweed,
Shells and stones,
Damp bathing suits
And ice-cream cones.

Waves pouring in
To a sand-castle moat.
Mend the defences!
Now we're afloat!
Water's for splashing,
Sand is for play,
A day by the sea
Is the best kind of day.

Shirley Hughes

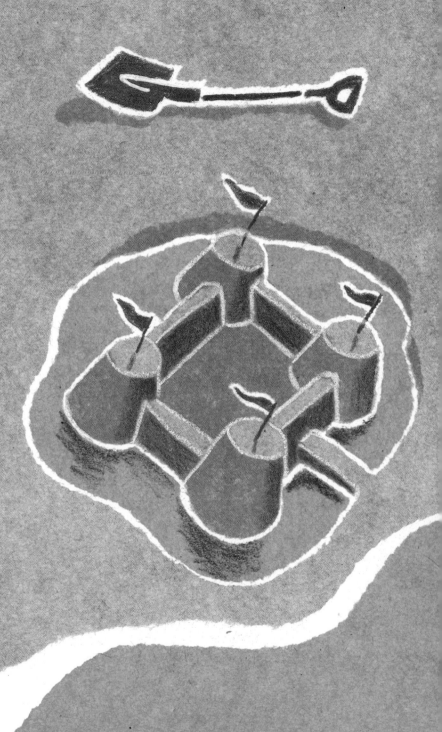

from **Cow in Meadow**

All day
In a leisurely, kindly sort of way
She crops, and chews the grass,
And watches children as they pass
Through gentle, placid, wondering eyes.
Daylong, under quiet skies . . .

All day she munches grass,
And munches grass,
Till the flies go
And evening shadows grow
And young boy's distant cry
'Coo-coo!' joins the rook-noise in the sky.
Then with a lurch she turns her head
Towards the cool, dark milking shed.

Clive Sansom

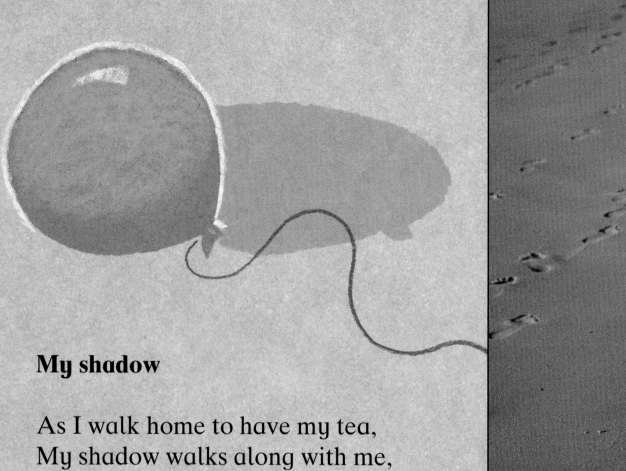

My shadow

As I walk home to have my tea,
My shadow walks along with me,
When I skip, then he skips too,
He copies everything I do.

I clap my hands, and his hands meet,
And just like me, he's got two feet,
I nod, he nods, it's such fun,
Playing with him in the sun.

As I walk home to have my tea,
The sun grows pale, and so does he,
And when the sun has gone from view,
I know that he will vanish, too.

Helen Russell

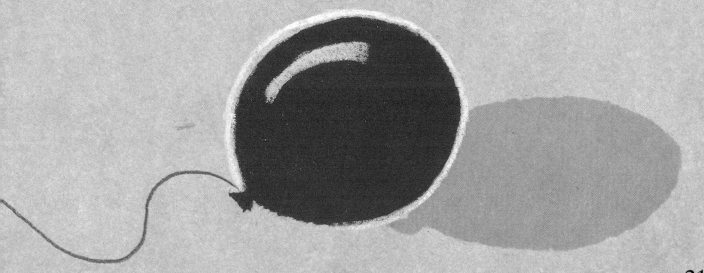

Stopping by Woods on a Snowy Evening

Whose woods these are I think I know.
His house is in the village though;
He will not see me stopping here
To watch his woods fill up with snow.

My little horse must think it queer
To stop without a farmhouse near
Between the woods and frozen lake
The darkest evening of the year.

He gives his harness bells a shake
To ask if there is some mistake.
The only other sound's the sweep
Of easy wind and downy flake.

The woods are lovely, dark, and deep,
But I have promises to keep,
And miles to go before I sleep,
And miles to go before I sleep.

Robert Frost

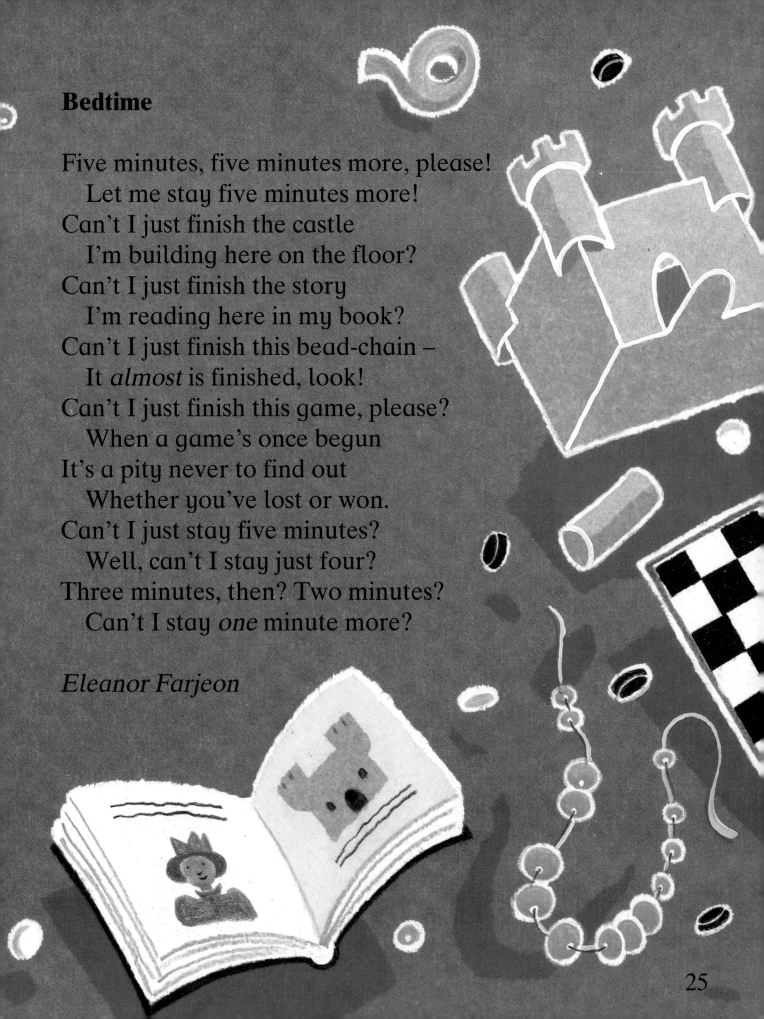

Bedtime

Five minutes, five minutes more, please!
    Let me stay five minutes more!
Can't I just finish the castle
    I'm building here on the floor?
Can't I just finish the story
    I'm reading here in my book?
Can't I just finish this bead-chain –
    It *almost* is finished, look!
Can't I just finish this game, please?
    When a game's once begun
It's a pity never to find out
    Whether you've lost or won.
Can't I just stay five minutes?
    Well, can't I stay just four?
Three minutes, then? Two minutes?
    Can't I stay *one* minute more?

Eleanor Farjeon

Bedtime Stories

"Tell me a story,"
Says Witch's Child.

"About the Beast
So fierce and wild.

About a Ghost
That shrieks and groans.

A skeleton
That rattles bones.

About a Monster
Crawly-creepy.

Something nice
To make me sleepy."

Lilian Moore

Night Fun

I hear eating.
I hear drinking.
I hear music.
I hear laughter.
Fun is something
Grownups never have
Before my bedtime.
Only after.

Judith Viorst

The Falling Star

I saw a star slide down the sky,
Blinding the north as it went by,
Too burning and too quick to hold,
Too lovely to be bought or sold,
Good only to make wishes on
And then forever to be gone.

Sara Teasdale

I'd Like To Be A Lighthouse

I'd like to be a lighthouse
    All scrubbed and painted white.
I'd like to be a lighthouse
    And stay awake all night
To keep my eye on everything
    That sails my patch of sea;
I'd like to be a lighthouse
    With the ships all watching me.

Rachel Field

How to use this book

Poetry is a very enjoyable area of literature and children take to it naturally, usually beginning with nursery rhymes. It's what happens next that can make all the difference! This series of thematic poetry anthologies keeps poetry alive and enjoyable for young children.

When using these books there are several ways in which you can help a child to enjoy poetry and to understand the ways in which words can be carefully chosen and sculpted to convey different atmospheres and meanings. Try to encourage the following:

- Joining in when the poem is read out loud.
- Talking about favourite words, phrases or images.
- Discussing the illustration and photographs.
- Miming facial expressions to suit the mood of the poems.
- Acting out events in the poems.
- Copying out the words.
- Learning favourite poems by heart.
- Discussing the difference between a poem and a story.
- Clapping hands to rhythmic poems.
- Talking about metaphors/similes eg what kind of weather would a lion be? What colour would sadness be? What would it taste like? If you could hold it, how would it feel?

It is inevitable that, at some point, children will want to write poems themselves. Writing a poem is, however, only one way of enjoying poetry. With the above activities, children can be encouraged to appreciate and delight in this unique form of communication.

Picture acknowledgements

APM cover; Eye Ubiquitous 5 (B Spencer), 12 (R Haynes), 16 (Paul Seheult); Life File 6/7 (Tim Fisher), 11 (Nicola Sutton), 14 (Nicola Sutton), 23 (David Heath); Telegraph Colour Library 8/9 (VCL), 21 (VCL); Tony Stone Worldwide 18/19 (Johan Elzenga), 28/29 (John Lund); Zefa 24.

Text acknowledgements

For permission to reprint copyright material the publishers gratefully acknowledge the following: Siv Cedering Fox, for 'In the Morning' by Siv Cedering Fox. Reprinted by permission of the author; Aileen Fisher for 'The Spinning Earth'; David Harmer for 'On A Blue Day'; Harper Collins UK for 'My Shadow' by Helen Russell from *Sit on the Roof and Holler* compiled by Adrian Rumble; Harper Collins US for 'Very Early' from *Dogs and Dragons, Trees and Dreams* by Karla Kuskin. Copyright © 1980 Karla Kuskin. Reprinted by permission of Harper Collins Publishers US; David Higham Associates for 'Bedtime' from *Silver Sand and Snow* by Eleanor Farjeon, published by Michael Joseph. 'Cow in the Meadow' from *An English Year* by Clive Sansom, published by Chatto and Windus. Reprinted by permission of David Higham Associates; 'Stopping by Woods on a Snowy Evening' from *The Poetry of Robert Frost* edited by Edward Connery Lathem. Copyright © 1951 Robert Frost. Copyright © 1969 by Henry Holt & Co. Inc. Reprinted by permission of Henry Holt & Co Inc. for Canadian rights and Random House UK for the British Commonwealth; Kids Can Press for 'My Own Day' from *Hey World, Here I Am* by Jean Little. Reprinted by permission of Kids Can Press Ltd, Toronto. Copyright © 1986 by Jean Little; Lescher & Lescher Ltd for 'Night Fun' from *If I Were in Charge of the World* by Judith Viorst; Random House UK for 'Washday' from *Singing Down the Breadfruit* by Pauline Stewart. Reprinted by permission of the publisher; Reed Consumer Books for 'I'd Like to be a Lighthouse' from *Taxis and Toadstools* by Rachel Field, published by William Heinemann Ltd; Scholastic Inc, for 'Bedtime Stories' from *Spooky Rhymes and Riddles* by Lilian Moore. Copyright © 1972 by Lilian Moore. Reprinted by permission of the publisher; Walker Books for 'Seaside' from *Out and About* by Shirley Hughes. Reprinted by permission of the publisher. While every effort has been made to secure permission, in some cases it has proved impossible to trace the copyright holders. The publishers apologise for this apparent negligence.

Index of first lines

King's Road Primary School
Rosyth - Tel: 313470